The Devil's Sonata

David Chorlton

FutureCycle Press
Mineral Bluff, Georgia

Published by FutureCycle Press
Mineral Bluff, Georgia, USA

ISBN 978-1-938853-05-0

Contents

III
Reading the Clouds

Thanks to Roberta for helping me learn about Tartini and baroque music, and for much more.

I

The Devil's Sonata

The Devil's Sonata

A stirring in the universe
suggests a theme. Cicadas have rosined their torsos
and keep all the world awake

except for a violinist
who dreams in sound. He lies
on a mattress stuffed with melodies

beside an unfinished letter to a friend
for whom the stars
are nails that hold the sky together,

yet something loosens
in the woven darkness. A melody
comes through the open window as gently

as a thief and flows through the room,
accessible only
to the dreamer, who luxuriates

in phrasing that sparkles in his mind
but turns to dust
when he wakes. He knows someone was here

playing with long fingers
on an instrument with light for strings,
and as virtuosity comes without practice to the Devil,

the signature is obvious. Now the work begins:
claiming his music
by writing notes in mortal time.

La Llorona

Beware the river, children; the river
with its icy teeth
and curses in the current
when it flows so quickly through
your sunlit days. It brings

water for the cottonwoods to grow
and give you shade; it comforts
you at night when it whispers
at the stars, but when
your mother walks
along its banks with her fingers

twisted in grief,
it rushes over rocks and swords
flash in the spray. Be good

to the river, children, for it cannot
change its course
and hates betrayal. Beware your mother,
children, for she has wept
the beauty from her face

and you are the last ones
she will ever cry for, resting
on the bed, beneath sheets
like silk rushing over you
where you wait
for her to join you soon.

Pimeria Alta

Once upon a barren time, a priest stood on the desert
with his arms set wide and crucified
on the light that streamed around him
and married the land to the one from which he had come.

He made of the sun a ring
to slip onto the fingers of ocotillo.
Then he knelt to pray

and darkness fell as a cloak on his back
as the bats streamed forth to drink from flowers
open for one night, throughout which
the scent was miraculous.
In the country of thorns

he lay down to sleep with a stone for a pillow
and dreamed a church to life
on dusty foundations with ornaments like snakes
climbing the altars. When mourning doves sounded the onset

of day, he drank from a pitcher of shadows
until it was dry as the earth.

The Discovery of Father Francisco Javier Saeta's Remains

There was little to collect.
Some bones and dried blood.
Many arrows.
The soldiers worked respectfully
as they scraped a long scream
from the whitewashed wall.

Coyote Run

At first he's a shadow bending
into an alley and stopping to look back
before darting out of sight
and then a flame of an animal
whose pelt is draped over his spine
trotting beside traffic
on a cloudy day when his eye
is bright like a jewel.
He's lost here. He's a splash
of wild graffiti on the air.
Nobody knows
what to do about him. We've all seen
the profiles on velvet-painted moons
and heard stories
about coyotes tricking fate
into submission. We've heard them
address the stars on intimate terms.
They slip in and out
of view, moving with ease
as they maneuver their bodies
between desert scrub and mythology.
Now one of them has come
to the center of our city, and he alone
knows how he got here. He's under watch
from the police, but he's fast
and fits into places where they can't follow.
No use shouting for him
to stop. He's a prayer turned carnivore,
a story passed in the oral tradition
to survive any fire,
and for us who plan each day,
he is imagination running off leash.

Coffee Stop

A harrier glides barely
higher than the grass between
December's dry mesquite
where the highway east of Tucson
dips beneath a desert wind.
It's time

for roadside coffee, so we turn
off to a café that stands alone
with the badlands ahead
and snow in the sky
to the south. Here the afternoon drama

plays on the inextinguishable TV
on the counter, as a lantern
of hope that we all
shall one day be beautiful
or brave

as Gary Cooper, whose photograph
hangs alongside Hopalong Cassidy
and the composite kitsch
with Indian, wolf and eagle
in fading rust and purple
while the cooler hums

its Coca Cola hum.
A reproduction cowboy
in his yellow slicker stands
with his horse at sunset
close to a late romantic

view of golden light with a colonial
church tower and a breath

of the Mexico we can
almost see as we step
outside beneath broken grays
and silver-edged clouds.

Lunchtime

When you stop for lunch in a landscape
three parts light to one of earth
with vegetation struggling to hold on
to the open space with mountains
pressing up from each horizon,
the wind blows cold across the table
next to yours as fragments
from the conversation drift: *You know*
there was never an armistice so legally
we're still at war with Germany,
a point which hasn't occurred to you
during the drive on dirt and asphalt,
but local politics can take a vicious turn,
especially when it comes to a candidate
for Sheriff who, in the event of Washington
calling for a gun grab, *won't obey*
but deputize everyone in Cochise County,
which, I'm reminded looking back
to the TV shows of years ago in England,
is Wyatt Earp country. Black hat, frock coat,
dark mustache, the farthest shooting gun
in the territory, the reluctant lawman
with a cause to justify every bullet fired
as if frontier justice were a blueprint
for foreign policy. Your sandwich is served
as a side dish to eavesdropping
on more complaints about all
the *radical extremists out there.*

Backyard Bird Count

Our back yard is a model of the world
from its arid region between the oleanders and the paloverde
to the strip of grassland running raggedly
beside the concrete drive where temperatures rise
to a hundred and twenty in June
and the wetlands near the dripping faucet
by the corner of the house
whose shadow creates a refuge
for pigeons when the desert comes to reclaim
what was once its own. We're counting sparrows

to ascertain how fast
the ice caps melt, watching a glacier diminish
surrounded by house finches, tracing deforestation
through frequent visits of the Cooper's hawk,
and measuring rising tides
where cormorants fly over on their way
to the lagoon in the local park. Weeds have taken over

what started as a lawn but the curve-billed thrasher
likes it bare; the palm tree by the back fence
died of thirst but the lovebirds
who belong in Africa still believe they're home;
there's a stump where the ornamental orange tree
gave up years ago but Inca doves flock
in its memory, and where the ground is covered by dead leaves
and decay the towhees scratch contentedly. We sit by the window

with a notebook in hand
watching for omens. Is the cactus wren's absence
from the front porch feeder a point from which the planet
can't return, or is the long-awaited sign
of ultimate survival the verdin
who comes every day to the snail vine?

dez-ert, *n.*

In winter the word
moves in shadow with one foot
placed hard on the earth
and the next just a light
gesture following. In spring

it's a flash
with a sword cutting through it
leaving half for an afterthought
when wildflowers fade.
There's a buzz

in the middle of summer
like a mouthful of bees
when the heat is a sting
with six letters
until rain falls

from a thunderclap
and an echo flows from the d
to the t. A desert
might be sand and stars;
it might be the space

where we fill in details
from the blue on a lizard's neck
to the phainopepla's crest
and the hook in the name
where it ends in a thorn.

The Deep Frozen Desert

(A copy of this poem was interred with legume seeds from the Boyce Thompson Arboretum at the Svalbard Global Seed Vault in Norway)

Beneath the ice light of the northern sky
in a mountain six hundred miles
from the nearest tree,
where frost runs deep into stone
and the only star is a signal
from a disappeared world

the seeds of a desert go along
the blue tunnel for storage
in a vault where they wait
for springtime to flower
from snowdrift and memory.
Here is mesquite and a crystal
of cold to preserve it; here

are prickly pear and sage
held in trust for the day
when the sun reappears; here
are agave and ironwood labeled
with ink that glows in the dark
like each golden segment
in the scorpion's tail

and the hourglass of fire
on the spider who crawls
between the stacks
of silver packages bearing
the indestructible seal
of night-blooming hope.

Wolf Politics

The wolf, having insufficient vocabulary
beyond the calls that leave a trail
of silver in the air, cannot understand
when it is spoken of as being expendable.
The wolf is a social animal

and has no room in its pack for division
between parties. It takes
what it needs but never has anything
left to collect interest. Wolf time

is the present moment, making platforms
or agendas irrelevant. To the wolf,
a kill is never veiled
in political justification. It does not
first deliberate, and afterwards
pretend remorse. A wolf

doesn't know its range
is disappearing until
there isn't anywhere to go
when it runs to the end of its breath.
Wolves have not romanticized their freedom,

they just hold on
to as much of it as they can.
It isn't easy

when politics comes down
to trading them away in a deal
from which nobody
can vote them back to life.

John Clare and the Desert

For a man who mourned an elm, a fallen saguaro
must be a sadness too. I've come to wonder
what John Clare would have thought
about the desert with its secret greens and brittle
edges. With his eye for the spider
on a Sunday walk, or for the Moorhen's nest
discovered among the roots of an old tree
on a riverbank, he surely would have bowed
to the scorpion or centipede to see
their luminous constructions, and been as thrilled
by a hawk's nest in the arms
of a tall cactus. He, who carried his melancholy self
outdoors, who was so dark inside
only the sun could save him, would not have balked
at summer mornings spent exploring
mesquite stands and arroyos
filling with heat. Watching doves and wagtails,
pewits and the swallow pair who nested
every year *beneath the freestone top,* he cared for them
while his contemporaries were building
smokestacks and factories and passing
Enclosure laws. He'd have put the Earth first here as well,
but he was sent in his time to a madhouse.
Nothing was too small for his attention,
from grasshoppers in spring to the polyanthus
spotted with dew. I'd offer him
some lizards with their scaled skins and eyes
seeming to sleep in their sockets, or the russet spot
on a verdin's wing. Then I imagine him stooping
to look for the next word in a line,
he who struggled in the world but lived in rhyme.

Reports from a Sky Island

I

A three-quarter moon floats free of the ridge
above swallowtails and sycamore
and the thirsty steps of deer that drum, stop
drum again through mesquite
where the odor from a days-old doe carcass
carries on a breeze as the vultures
we disturbed fly dripping
offal from their beaks
down between the ants along the path
processing from last light into dark.

II

Sounds at night
ring clearly from the drilling
insect calls to the whip-poor-will's
three syllables connecting
grasses with the stars.

III

Soaking in the light beside a velvet ash
a snake has curled into an arabesque
but quickly stretches to full length
and disappears between two stones
in the seconds
it takes for the earth
to swallow the long geometry
of brown and yellow scales.

IV

Two life zones connect
in the cottonwoods
where a yellow-billed cuckoo
calls from the Upper
toward the slope where Lower
Sonoran begins in the fading blooms
of ocotillo against the hot June sky.

V

The flies assembled
above the water at the mouth
to the abandoned mineshaft
create an electronic buzz
made louder in the confines
of rock walls overshadowing
a warning not to enter
and the columbines that lean
into the cool air passing
from a deep, damp journey
into light.

VI

A whiskered screech-owl's first
call vibrates softly
against the edge of light.

Repeat Exposure

The first time you look
out of the cabin window you see
a wide green shadow
arched across the stream. The next time

it seems more earth than leaves
and drier than you thought.
You go back a third time

having come to love the sounds
that rise at night
from the undergrowth
and the long notes of the owls
waiting in the dark.
It becomes a highlight

of the year to open the door
and watch the birds loop
after flies. Everything is
familiar now, from the smooth rock
on the right bank

to the tree roots holding
to the left, and the mesh
of fine branches as the oaks recede
behind the sycamores.
One time in spring

light breaks from the ground
and in winter
there's a pale glow

to the chill. Now it's summer once
again, the redstarts
come and go, and the evergreens
open up their secrets
to you, who they have eventually
learned to trust.

Desert Black

A rattlesnake slides at the tip of a storm
through the shivering grass
with two drops of alertness in his eyes
and a lightning strike coiled
in his mouth. He's minutes ahead of the rain

rolling down from the mountain
that's turning dark as the thunder in the clouds.
And he's hungry like the sky

when it consumes the desert's light.

Four Windows

Webs of cold hang between the junipers
where jays and juncos dust
snow from the branches as more snow
falls to replace it. If frost
had a heart it would fly
through the brittle spaces
where dormant grass spikes through
the gathering drift.

*

A chair toppled back by last night's wind
lies not far from the wood pile
where pine siskins perch between flights
to the column of seed that sustains them.
An old metal bed frame
next to the fence holds a chill
in its legs that runs deep
into the ground beneath.
And the soft net falls
with only the flash
in a flicker's red wing to relieve it.

*

Some gnarled stems of cactus resist
the process that takes
away shapes
and makes of the frost a whisper
passing the secret through forest
of what it is the lock on the shed door
protects with its tooth biting into the cold.

*

Little remains past the screen
but the dip in the road where it points
toward the peak that disappeared
some hours ago when the silence
came to erase it.

The House George Walker Built

We're in a ghost town as December draws
to a close. It's cold
outside where the wind is combing
snow from Silver Peak. The house
in which we sleep is old
and has walls within walls where at night
animals climb through the spaces between,
glad for the warmth from a fire burning
down to an old year's ash.

II

Storm Warnings

Picacho Motel

The sunlight checks in
to the Picacho Motel
late in the afternoon
and enters a room
through the space an air conditioner
left in the wall after coughing
out its last cold breath.
The big sign above the parking lot
casts the same shadow
it did when its faded paint
was fresh and blue
as desert sky. In passing,
from the interstate
anyone can see the sadness
pressing up against the doors
and the boarded up
windows a guest might once
have cracked open
to listen to the stars
move across the sky. This place
used to be a comma marking time
to pause for breath,
never the period at journey's end;
now it's just
space between the lines
in a story about the day
power was cut and for the first
time the lamps
around the empty parking lot
stayed dark when a coyote
came on ghost steps to sniff
the ground, knowing no more
than the scent
that accompanies decline and fall.

Alaskan Miniatures

I

Snow clings to time
and rock beneath the clouds
where long rivers end
their journeys into light.

II

The fine green rain
in the forest
is to water
what the ferns are
to the trees.

III

A cellist with a snow cap
at each shoulder
plays with an eagle at the tip
of the bow
he draws slowly across
the low clouds.

IV

A woodpecker drums into the silence
trapped beneath
a spruce's bark.

V

Late on a summer night
a blush passes over
the forests across the sound
as a chill whets the peaks
to a sharper edge.

VI

A winter wren flies
between trees so close
together there
is no space for shadows.

VII

A raven at the crossroads
looks both ways: toward
the poles the Tlingit made

and at the cross
above the church in which
the Russians prayed.

VIII

An hour before midnight
the water is still pale in the cove
where darkness is moored.

Seeing Sitka

The battleground is quiet today
with water lapping at the shore
and low cloud in the trees
where the natives once lost
in hours what had taken centuries
to build. There's light rain

at the moment, clearing later
to reveal the mountains. No trace
remains of the disease
the invaders introduced,
just their church
in which the prayers begged for a cure

and when it arrived
the natives prayed there too
to thank the new god
for saving them. The forecast
used to be for showers
of smallpox followed

by the scent of incense
though the weather doesn't change
by more than a few degrees
from day to day while the seasons
float up and down the sound
behind the ships

that stop here now.
Their passengers disembark
for a few hours before
sailing on with their souvenirs
into the short hours of darkness
when an eagle folds the night away

beneath his wings. He's perched
above the road
that runs along the edge of land
where the Bishop's house recalls
the time of porcelain settings
on the table with the samovar

when the talk was of trading
for the rubel, before
it made way for the dollar,
but whatever the flag the true
currency was always fur
torn from animals' backs.

Varied Thrush

In a silence so tall
trees disappear
into rain

and compass needles
all point toward
the sky,

the Devil's club collects
whatever light
passes through

when the clouds break
to drift out
on the slow tide

and in
on the back of a shower.
Fallen trunks

press their mossy,
broken weight
between the ferns

that grow
like whispers
from wet shadows.

When a thrush
calls once, a rock
splits open

and a tree roots
in the moisture
in the cleft. When

it calls twice,
the forest turns a shade
darker than before,

and with the third
call comes
the landing

on a stump for long
enough to see
the breast stripe

and the eye
that blinks
before the atmosphere

absorbs it.

One Hundred Fifteen Degrees

We can't see the desert from the city
but we feel it
on days like today when the temperature
at ten a.m. is a hundred
dry degrees promising trouble
later on. After the hundred and ten
at noon, everybody counts
each additional degree all the way
to the day's high as if
at this point extra heat
makes any difference,
while we could be talking
about one more candidate for the presidency
being intolerable, bemoaning
every new cut in spending for schools
or lamenting the latest
casualty in the foreign war. Keeping
to the weather makes for calm
conversation between strangers, holding us
back from, for instance, discussing
climate change and polar bears
and questioning what
the loss of one more would mean.
Such talk would be a waste of time. You'd have
to ask the polar bear.

*

The Dow went up one hundred and forty-five points
today, while the heat
remained as it has been
and will be
through the coming cloudless days
during which the forecasters will indicate
on a map of the state
which forests are burning

and which can yet be saved
when the monsoon begins. It's easy to measure
losses and gains
when numbers stand in line
for an easy overview,
the way rainfall amounts would be shown
if there were any, but by the end
of the dry season
there is no index to show
whether junipers or oaks
went down most in the fires.

*

Days like this come every summer,
setting records
for next year to beat.
We'll be waiting
with a garden hose to keep the trees alive
and pouring water
on the vines. Nothing much
will change: leaves will curl
at their edges, plantings will be limp,
and when sparrows bathe
in the dust, it will cloud up and sparkle
like drops of thirst in the light.

Night Findings

Derobrachus hovorei

The saw teeth shine along the antennae
on a beetle that grows at every sighting.
It bores through the warmth on a July night
the way it bores through a paloverde's roots
while the gloss matures on its military shell.

It's black sweat on the darkness.
It's black as fear when it flies

before touching down on the driveway
with a pinch of moonlight
between its trembling mandibles.

Anaxyrus microscaphus

Between the sunset and the rain,
against a wall of distant thunder,
where water is a shallow dream,
toads expand their vocal sacs
and the silence of the night
creaks open on an unoiled hinge.

Periplaneta americana

After a day in moist seclusion,
cockroaches enter their time,

exploring the minutes
inside a clock

that glows in the dark.
When they fly, they are flakes,

of amber crackling
like paper castanets.

Hemidactylus turcicus

When the geckos come out from the doorframe,
they enter a vertical world
in which they climb
on any surface, with their pale spotted skins
soft to the touch and transparent. Even in storms,
their bones are lightning
flashing inside them.

Storm Warnings

The urban sunlight hits a black wall moving
in from the desert
where nothing has moved
since a roadrunner
spun around and ran for cover,
finding none. Not even the frail

mesquite gives shade
and neither is the dry earth
a comfort. Suddenly
the wind digs underneath it
until darkness has risen
to such a height
that its progression from open space

to city comes
as the portent of a thirst
so vast it leaves everyone
created equal.

*

The sky is a balance sheet
with anvil clouds to the east
and sunset in the west.
Markets have been threatening all day
to collapse

but a shy wind of hope
runs through the closing figures
although the first lightning
finds nobody prepared. Each flash

stills all activity,
and the false prophets can't say
which way we should run.

*

Restless dogs are circling our beds,
looking for somewhere to hide.
They feel the pressure falling
but don't understand why.
Dogs don't understand money either;

the dollar and the yen
are all the same to them,
especially when there's thunder
rattling the windows
and we

can only listen and say
it's all right, just lie down and sleep,
while we can't sleep ourselves
for wondering

whether the exchange rate for lightning
is in our favor tonight.

Birds from the Interstate

Amid the sparse mesquite
all that moves
is a roadrunner
as he darts a stretch
then stops and darts again,
chasing the heat in a circle.
There's a brown-speckled breeze
in his feathers,
and his crest
points straight at the sun.

A freight train hauls a new shipment
from China past a flat
expanse of desert, where cracks
have risen to the surface
and the saguaros are riddled
with gunshot and drought.
They lean left and right
but grip the earth as gently
as white-winged doves grip them

when they perch at the tip
overlooking the land
on which billboards begin
by selling bets
as dice roll away from the road
in a casino cut
from raw chance and artificial lights,

then progress from
Marine recruiting
to redemption
to offering deals
that flash past too quickly
to read, while the ravens

who circle above them
want nothing
except the air and a place
to rest and caw black folly
at everything beneath them.

What Comes

When you live close to nature, you take what comes.
—Tom Beatty, Miller Canyon, Arizona

It might be a Lucifer hummingbird
whose gorget shines magenta
against apples ripening
on trees in August's orchard
that you see, or else

a family from Oaxaca
who made it this far and chose the wild
canyon after crossing over
and who stop
when you encounter them,
frightened as the ocelot

a dog treed here in spring.
If you look the other way
to let them pass,
you'll notice how the cliff wall
seems to hang
between the sky and the oaks

while at the saddle
between two peaks
aspens are absorbed by clouds
one day and by smoke
on another. When what comes

is fire, it is never in the forecast.
It just begins
and strips
a mountain to the bone.
When you live where the border
between good weather and bad

is harder to cross
than the one between countries,
it might be the black flood you hear
washing away the thrush's call
and taking back
everything the golden days

delivered. What comes is yours
to keep: as much a part of you
as the shiver in the blade
is of the axe.

Album of Fire

Winston Lewis' Photographs

I

A dark cloud fans
open from a ridge
pulsing fire
as if the mountain
could spread wings
to escape.

II

Some green still highlights
the foreground
where oaks remain
while beyond them the slopes
are burned dry
and shadows move across them
like a wounded creature's tongue.

III

The pale, pointed fronds
crumpled on a yucca stem
point in all directions
to indicate
where the flames ran to
when they were finished here.

IV

After the burn
a soft light returns
to the familiar peak,
whose contours alone
remain unchanged.

V

So many trees
with ash for leaves.

VI

An inquisitional glow
springs out along the canyon
where the owls
have lost their way.

VII

From the high ridge on a clear day
smoke has the elegant sweep
of a silk scarf
waved with abandon.

VIII

On the night of full moon
a tide of bright red
flows up toward the stars
from a brush of fresh watercolor
across a wet page.

IX

Even the long-awaited rain
follows the creek bed
with a black rush
and nothing to slow it down.

Letter from Among the Pines

To whom it may concern: the acorn
woodpeckers are still
calling from the boughs where
sunlight illuminates rough bark
and plumage. So many centuries
have flown between these trees,
time no longer casts a shadow
on the fallen leaves and needles
crackling underneath our steps
when we climb to see the valleys
spin around us, in and out
of sunsets, cutting deeper
in the earth, and shading
into sky. The ravens call
the way they used to
when the Sinagua people listened
before they bundled their possessions
and walked to the edge of the world,
which in their time
was not far. We're listening
for thunder, watching the daily
massing of clouds. Will it rain?
Will the Steller's jays return
from wherever they went?
Was a lost tribe waiting
for them there? When did the pygmy
nuthatches arrive
to tap at the trunks
and to dart so close
as to render us inanimate
where we sit through the slow
afternoon? This is just a record
of our presence, who spent
some days between the early

morning chatter and the crickets
rubbing up against the darkness,
making sounds reminiscent
of the shells rattling
on Indian dancers' legs.

Creation Stories

When the earth was shivering,
the people who had made it
added grass and trees and bushes
to keep it warm. That was easy.
Then they found it was weak and talked
about the problem before deciding
to make mountains and rocks, which they called
bones. But the earth couldn't breathe,
so thunder was invoked. Just like that, as if all
it took was to wave a hand
and there were storms
with cleansing rains and lightning.
Next came the sun, from east to west,
but too low so it scorched all it passed
and the people had to crawl
on hands and knees to stay low enough
to avoid it, until fine tuning
raised it to its best position in the sky.
The moon was a problem.
It made the nights too light.
Up and up it went
to where it gazed from among the stars,
and the nights became dark. The story
showed creation to be simple, from the first
declaration of a site in the universe
to the picking of fruits
that made it all good. Then the time arrived
to tell a different one, in which
the rivers flowed away and could not be caught,
the snow turned into wings and lifted
from the mountaintops, and a dry wind
blew across the earth, the origins
of which became the cause
for many years of talking, talking, and more

talking, in which time the birds
flew away to look for another earth,
which did not exist, and when the talking
ended there was a silence
which begged for the story to begin again
but in a different version,
and the arguing began over which one to use.
While this continued
the earth grew smaller, and the smaller
it became the more hostile
was the bickering over whether it was better
to go back to the way the Apache
had built the earth, or to turn to the Tohono O'odham
whose First Born started out with algae
from which everything took form.
I like that one, someone said, but no one else
agreed. So it went on, story after story
was considered. *How much will it cost?*
How long will it take? How soon can we build our factories
again? The ones with the stories
couldn't answer, so none was chosen
and there was only the darkness on the water
from the first time.

Touching Darkness

I

It takes the insects years
to journey through the fallen sycamore
in lush
late summer grass
beside the trail at thunder's edge
where night moves slowly
up canyon
and the broken trunk of an oak
fills with webs and darkness.

II

The grays above the juniper
range from pale
to the metallic
shade of dusk, drawn along
a ridge that darkens until darkness
is a sound
after every other sound subsides.

III

Water in the mine
carries darkness deep
into the mountain nobody has entered
since a warning sign
was posted at the mouth
and flows out of the silence
just enough to reach the place
where sunlight leans
against the columbines.

IV

Through an eye that opens after sunset
the bats stream all
along the canyon, as if
infinity had wings. Sometimes lightning
from above the mountain
flashes to reveal
their faces when
they hover
at a moment's nectar.

Broken

Whatever we've grown to think is solid and strong and durable is under siege. The threats are mounting. The evil is growing. Darkness is falling. —Glenn Beck

Each time the telephone rings
it's someone saying *Please
send money we need to mend
another broken piece of the world*
and each time we say *We're sorry
we can't help but good luck*
then the news comes on the radio
with the daily list of unsolved
problems from the revolution in one
country to the riots in another
all of which leaves us feeling
as weary as our refrigerator
which can't keep up
with the hottest August ever
so we go to the industrial zone
to look for a replacement
among the born-again appliances
standing in rows in the sun
or inside a space too large
for the ceiling fan to cool
as it spins and rattles and manages
to somehow hold on
without ever falling
from its place as a symbol
of good intentions not really
helping but never running down
or away from the place
history assigned it.

Chiricahua September

Entering Paradise

The low mountains press
their shadow sides against
descending clouds
as rain slaps between yucca
where a falcon peels
from the dark sky
and into stubble
before the shower soaks back
into grays broken only
by swallows and lightning.
There's a crackle in the west
and forks stabbing down
behind the cattle guard sign,
and the road runs
slowly along
the edge of light
that moves off to the east
from one fencepost to the next,
dips beneath a mourning dove
then turns toward the twilight
climbing Silver Peak
whose every tree and stone
is another shade of thunder.

Roost

Forty vultures roost
beneath the open sky
on the dead trees
across the creek, sleeping
black against black
through the night rain
falling between flashes
in the storm. Nothing

moves them from their boughs.
They are hunched
like prophets resigned
to their doom, until
they spread their wings wide
as if the rising sun
had pinned them
to the daylight.

After Rain

A pale wash of cloud
lies over the peaks
and the slopes shade
green to green
from ocotillo
to the juniper
where a bead of sap
shines in the bark.

Parabacillus hesperus

An insect too thin
for any name but its Latin one
grips the fine mesh
on the porch screen, backlit
by a mountain
against which it is
a compass needle pointing
to the spirit world.

Last Light

Silver Peak slips into moonlight
with silence for a crest
and the mountainous calm
of the day's last breath
pressing into the earth.

Late Summer Storm

With one broken yellow and two
straight white lines to guide it,
the road disappears
into narrowing perspective
and low cloud
closing in along the wires
where kingbirds watch
the darkening air for insects
while the mountains disappear
from around them. The landscape
becomes a tumbling scale of shades
sliding across each other
as a curtain of hail
rattles the asphalt free of the ground
and the sky is drawn
like a handkerchief through a ring
for a trick
in which all things are changed;
even the stalk of a yucca
is a lightning flash with roots.
Between land
and sky, no boundary
exists; the distant
now is close at hand; the future
flows toward us
at the speed of water
when the earth is too hard
for it so soak in.

III

Reading the Clouds

After Reading Larkin

The ashtrays are full in Larkin's hotel
and the lamps don't make light
but a mood
for absences that occupy the rooms
whose doors face each other
across a silent corridor. Goodnight England

and goodnight trains
that blaze into the night
with a heartbeat never slowing.
Goodnight Larkin. Goodnight travelers

going back in time. Goodnight
to those who never stop
complaining. They read the sports page
first and leave the rest behind.
I'm becoming more like them each day

but I live where the sky is wide
and loneliness likes
confined spaces best. When I write
to find words for what's wrong

there's a list as varied as the samples
Larkin's salesmen carried
in a suitcase, and I'll accept
any opportunity to unpack them. Here
are the brokers of war, the merchants

who wrap their goods in a flag
and animals in cages waiting
for their turn to be the experiment
that helps manufacture a drug

so new there is no disease for it to cure.
That's just a start. Would you like

to see more? I've got time
and I'm not selling anything. I just want
you to know.

Coming Summer

The geckos come out from cracks
in the house walls where
warmth soaked through their skins in winter
and cling like condensation
to the ceiling of the porch,
pale in the white light the lamp
by the door spills across them.
They are the portent of a summer

through which the lost will wander
and evaporate inside their clothes;
when the print on maps will fade in the sun
before anyone can read directions;
when the round Earth will give way
to a flat one that tilts
into hallucination. What is distant
will appear as close at hand

from the break in the horizon
where smugglers carry their backpacks
to the end of a road
whose white lines curl back
to tie a knot for the union
of poverty and risk. Those with money
will place it in cold storage

while those without
will be armed and ready but have
no one to turn on
but themselves. They will be shown
on late night television
between the game show and the infomercial

selling instructions for success
at a price rising with the temperature.

Cheap Mangos

There's an easy flow of music through
the speakers at the supermercado
where papayas ripen while you watch
their skins disintegrate
the way a man's skin does
when he's found on his back in the desert
facing the sun with his mouth locked
between a scream and a prayer. His trouser leg
is torn where a coyote
came to gnaw at his thigh
and of his right forearm only
the bones remain, while on his left wrist
a watch still measures time.
The music has a teardrop in its beat
and nostalgia in the singer's voice,
but the juice aisle is a happy place
with any flavor you'd remember
from a trip across the border
going south to a colorful village
with peppers stacked in the market
just like these red, green, yellow ones
displayed in the order of their bite,
a village likely similar
to one the woman left
whose sweater clings to what remains
of her where she collapsed
in a pair of sports shoes good for many
more miles with the tread on their soles
and Just Do It style. Something pulled at her hair
where her scalp peeled away,
but the strap on her brassiere
is indestructible as the belt
that falls slack where the flesh has wasted
from her hips. Had she made it

to a road she might have found
her way to Phoenix, to the store
where the cakes in the cold case
are churrigueresque and mangos
are two for ninety-nine cents.

A Response to the Man on the Bus

Whoever you are
with the Navajo face
who, between Seventh Street and Third,
gave me your essay
about the Chief on a red horse
and corn pollen memories
from before the white man
arrived; was it because I sat reading
while the other passengers talked into their cell phones
that you chose me? You couldn't have known
my book was Vaclav Havel's *The Power of the Powerless*
when you unfolded the sheet
with your words describing fighter jets
flying over sacred ground
and the cement block walls hiding views
that once were wild. You took your seat
and stared ahead through the wide front window
at the long perspective
of a street that once had been
a desert, and I saw the resentment
passing all the way to the tips of your braids. You wrote,
we aren't here to benefit your consumption
in a country whose official language is advertising.
Then you got off
and walked to the light rail stop
in a way that made everyone around you
look as if we didn't belong, aliens all
inside our own skins.

Letter to Donald Locke

Dear Donald, When we talked again by phone after such
a long time, it felt like completing sentences
begun twenty years back
as we turned to Cezanne and you asked
What did he see, what did Cezanne see? as if more
than art depended on it. We have a few of his paintings
and four drawings at the museum here, close enough
for me to visit for a few more weeks, and I just came
from staring at them. He saw
trees leaning toward the paper's edge
trying to find their place, and he saw empty space
as his closest ally in the quest
for balance. In the pencil strokes and sparse
brushwork on a white sheet, you can feel
the waiting it took to decide what came next.
Such nervous patience took years
to control. If ever two dimensions had a servant
it was Cezanne, for whom the edges
of a canvas were the law. We ask
what he saw, because so much is withheld
and we can never know what was omitted to make
space for the mountain. His restraint
is what stays with me most. All the more in our age
of special effects and gimmicks like covering a river
and calling it art. And the subtle tension
in the moment he stopped painting
is still thrilling. There's a still life with a white cloth
whose folds dissolve without completion
and it rests quietly against a gray
that won't reveal what it was, but the lost edges
are the ones that hold attention. As I looked at it
I heard Cezanne's footsteps backing away
the moment he knew there was nothing
to add. There was a red step

and a blue one, then the click
the door made. *What did he see?* Was it order? Was it
that nothing in nature exists in isolation? Or is the question
What did he know? and the answer: *Whatever you see you must
make it into what it needs to be.*

New York City Skyline

From floor seventeen through the window screen
the view is of towers and spires
and windows growing smaller
until the eye no longer finds
details on the slender shapes that turn
into a bouquet of lights at dusk. Millions live

within the frame. Their cars honk impatiently.
Sirens tell them help is on the way. They walk.
They speak the official language
of somewhere else, climb stairs, ride
elevators up and down and crowd

the underground. One of them
is the golden man whose clothes, shoes, cap
and skin are painted so he glows
all the way from Bleecker Street to Broadway
to wherever he goes at the end of the line
where he is last to leave his seat and walk
inconspicuously home. Nobody stares

at him here or cares
what color he is when he sleeps.
The sky returns early morning with its light
and a hurry in each pair of shoes. From up here
morning prayers and hangovers
look the same. You can't tell

an executive going out to spend
a million from the man who steps out from the crowd
to reach into a trash bin and pluck
out a chocolate pastry
without ever breaking his stride.

Summer Scenes of Fire and Oil

I

As he walks, a man in the forest
looks to the ground
although the black trunks are still tall
and recall their silver days
of pointing to the sky.

II

A pelican has opened its oily beak
and lifted itself up
from the sand, turning
toward the deceptive reflections
on the surface of the sea.

III

One cross holds firmly
to the small dome on the blue tower
while the other has begun to lilt
as the wood gives way beneath it
and trees in the churchyard lean
with a warning to run
if there is anywhere to run toward.

IV

Fishes wash ashore like broken
rainbows. A gull on its back
flaps in the oil
and cannot understand
why water is heavy when
the sky is so bright.

V

Preserved fruit in the cellar
survived the blaze. It's being raised now
from the ash. Some memories
are kept in air-tight jars.

VI

The turtle on the beach has exhausted
its strength and stopped
dead in its slow tracks
like a breath
that turned black.

VII

Some men in a small town sit
on a stone bench and wait
for the smoke to pass when that is all
there is to do except to light
another cigarette.

VIII

The dragonfly holds its long blue torso
straight and steady
as it tries to clean its wings
on marsh grass
where drops of water hang.

IX

With a metal relic in her hand
and icons in her lap,
an old woman from the wooden age
watches her village being taken
in smoke while she speaks back
to a god who has spoken first.

X

A crumpled gannet lies with its head
too heavy for its neck
and its wings
spread like a hand of cards
a gambler threw down
when he lost.

The Helicopter at 2 a.m.

Sometime between the dream
and the drink of water it begins,
coming close and louder
then fading as it reaches
the far point of its circle
and returning overhead. The light beam

sweeps through the alleys
and the helicopter clings
desperately to the sky. What does it want?
Is it searching for the mockingbird
who sings all night? Did somebody
escape from uniformity?
Is a census being held of those
who sleep beneath the stars?
Perhaps it's looking for
a trace of radiation from Japan

or the lost people
who lived here before
the men with Colt revolvers arrived,
who never saw
the white light from the sky
coming toward them, or heard
the future's growling voice.

Museum of Solitude

You'll feel the silence rubbing
up against you like a cat
when you've got nothing to feed either one.
Not a word. Not a scrap.
Here's a Russian poet's room
with a kettle, a cup,
a shelf with some books,
a chair and a shawl
to cover the upholstery's holes.
Is it cold? Yes, it's cold.
But there's tea
and a faucet to run to drown
out the sound when you talk.
You must see the carriage
from the train bound for exile.
Its windows are black, it never
comes back, and a few sad belongings
are wrapped in a sack. Clickety-clack,
you can listen all night
to the wheels on the track
and your face will age fast
so nobody knows
when you get there
who you are. Here is the wall
where mothers would wait
to visit their sons, and the guard
at the gate with his gun. You can sit
in a cell and stop time. Here is the file
in which your appeal
has been waiting for years
to be read, and the notepad for writing
down dreams at the side of the bed.
By the mirror a cloth
has the power to erase, when the nights

never end, your quicksilver face.
Once you're in here
you stay and keep counting the days
as they come and they go and the answer,
whatever you ask,
is officially no.

To the Man on Death Row, Waiting

It's a fine day
with the air being clear after recent rain
and a coolness now the long
summer has ended. I'm looking at a picture
of the room prepared
for your final breath, with its bar of artificial light
above a kind of bed set
with sheets as if it were in a hospital
you would be in to be healed, and the long
dark window on the other side
of which the seats are empty now.
The walls could be beige, almost
a color, as if blue or green
would have been more than you deserved.
It's after three, the trees outside here
are filled with birdsong, and in the distance
is the long, repeated note
of the whistle on a freight train gathering speed
for the miles of desert
it will cross before nightfall.
Nobody knows yet
whether this is your final day, with all
the appeals and last minute attempts
to keep you alive, but whether or not
tomorrow happens I hope
you enjoyed the fried okra, steak well done,
ice cream and Dr. Pepper drink. I'm listening
to the radio for news amid that of the killing
in war that goes on every day
for word that one death
will be avoided. Looking out
at the winter lawns beginning to sprout along
our street, and the shadows
lengthening across them, it is hard

to imagine the world reduced to a room, and time
to a countdown. Clear skies tonight, the forecast says,
and fine tomorrow, when the train
will be crossing Texas with a rumble like a thousand
hearts determined never to stop.

6:22 p.m.

I knew there would be days like this:
the clock crawling across the wall,
depression in the sky,
only memories to fill the time
I hoped to use for writing,

so I leave the silence
to speak for itself
and submit a blank page
to which I sign my name,

noting the time exactly
when the first drop of darkness
falls in the yard where the birds
have been calling
since dawn.

Reading the Clouds

The west has a gilded edge today,
and the east is a whisper of darkness.
To the north, just a few
thin streaks drift over
the meeting of desert and mountains,

while patches of violet
mark the route to the border and beyond.
A scent of rain
comes to the city, beneath its solid layer
of introspection
the hour before the mockingbirds
roost and the geckos

crawl out through the cracks
in our door frame. Another day
turns to a late splash of romance
before the dark. Then the accountants
of life and death lick the tips of their pens
to prepare the entries:

four hundred-and-fifty to earthquake,
three to an unmarked grave,
a bird set free after rescue,
two lost dogs found,
and a bomb dismantled
that might have left even them
too filled with mourning to keep count.

Omen

A nervous wind blows down the street,
pushing up against each door
and rapping branches on the windows.
It carries a wave of dust

that yellows the air and obscures
the afternoon sky. Nobody goes to answer
when it knocks; nobody wants
to let it inside. It rattles and rushes

and rustles the trees where the grackles
are coming to roost. It must be a portent
for darker than usual news; a message
sent ahead of its messenger; the displacement

of air caused by the wing of a bird
about to grow extinct.

Night Transport

When a truck passes in the night
our headlights shine through the holes
in its silver side
to illuminate the bodies
of cattle cramped inside
while their moans soak into the traffic noise
and, having overtaken, the vehicle
displays its rear
adorned with cowboy-sized letters
vertically arranged
to spell out
B H
L O
E P
S E
S
E
D

End of the Line

Another man too poor to fail
sits down to occupy
a few square feet of sunlight
on a warm November day
at the light rail station
where the fare is a dollar
and seventy-five cents for a short
or a long ride; it's all the same
to the machine that takes the money
and to anyone without sufficient change
to spend on a ticket, even if
he had somewhere to go
after he's spoken with the officer
who stopped to ask
why he sits here with no apparent
intent to move along. There is nobody
present for him to disturb.
Nobody to be offended
by the way he smells.
Nobody who complained
about the way he stretches his legs
across the platform
or spreads his arms wide,
leaning back in a manner to suggest
he's relaxed. He hasn't asked
anyone for a donation, hasn't made
promises about an interest rate,
hasn't paid for a vacation
with someone else's savings, hasn't
started any wars in recent history,
and he never hired help
at sub-survival wages. He just happens
to be here, on public display,
for the passengers on the next train

to see as they pass through,
what anyone might look like soon.
Nobody needs to travel
any further to see the end of the line.
It's right here,
resisting arrest.

At This Same Time

Before dawn, before the truck
moves slowly along the street with newspapers,
before the first chattering sparrows
in the oleanders, before the coffee
and the growling lawn mowers next door, before
the lights are turned on in the cold,
before business, before money,
before trash pickup and restaurants, when
the only borders were horizons
and rivers spoke in free flow, before
buying and selling and gunfire,
before contracts, before time
had been broken into increments
and moved between Heaven and Earth,
there was darkness here; only
the stars were more brilliant
before gods, before dawn.

The Bat God

With wings of silk and a velvet mask
he hangs in a recess
until the dark is thick enough to stir

then the blood flows faster
to his ears
and they open to receive the music
made by stars. He's a memory

that can't find a way
back into the mind. Imagine a wolf's heart

shrunken to fit
inside a tiny breast; imagine
a flame as a tooth. When you wake up
in the small hours

thirsty for light
and reach for the switch, he'll be there,
he'll be silence

with an edge so sharp
It cuts. Imagine navigating
fear with a map you can touch
but not see; imagine

your reflection flying
from the mirror

and never coming back.

Acknowledgments

Grateful acknowledgment is made to the following publications in which these poems first appeared, some in slightly different versions:

Avocet: "John Clare and the Desert"
The Blue Guitar: "Repeat Exposure," "Alaskan Miniatures," "Seeing Sitka,"
    "One Hundred Fifteen Degrees," "Birds from the Interstate,"
    "Touching Darkness," "Late Summer Storm"
Blue Collar Review: "The Helicopter at 2 am"
Blue Unicorn: "Pimeria Alta"
Boyce Thompson Arboretum Newsletter: "The Deep Frozen Desert"
Brevities: "The Discovery of Father Francisco Javier Saeta's Remains"
Chiron Review: "To the Man on Death Row, Waiting"
Edgz: "6:22pm"
Minotaur: "Coming Summer"
The New Verse News: "Lunchtime," "Wolf Politics," "Summer Scenes of
    Fire and Oil," "What Comes"
Parting Gifts: "Coyote Run"
Pembroke Magazine: "The House George Walker Built," "Backyard Bird
    Count"
Pemmican: "Museum of Solitude," "A Response to the Man on the Bus"
Poem: "The Devil's Sonata," "Desert Black," "Reading the Clouds"
Presa: "Four Windows"
Skidrow Penthouse: "After Reading Larkin," "End of the Line"
Slipstream: "New York City Skyline," "Cheap Mangos," "At This Same
    Time"
Stride: "de-zert, *n.*," "The Bat God"
Third Wednesday: "Coffee Stop," "Reports from a Sky Island," "Varied
    Thrush," "Night Findings," "Storm Warnings," "Broken," "Picacho
    Motel," "Album of Fire," "Letter from Among the Pines," "Creation
    Stories," "Chiricahua September"
Voices on the Wind: "Letter to Donald Locke," "Omen," "Night Transport"

*Cover art, "Treble Clef Barnstar" by Sven Manguard; photo of the author
by Roberta Chorlton; cover and interior book design by Diane Kistner
(dkistner@futurecycle.org); Adobe Garamond Pro text with Sovba titling*

About FutureCycle Press

FutureCycle Press is dedicated to publishing lasting English-language poetry and flash fiction books, chapbooks, and anthologies in both print-on-demand and ebook formats. Founded in 2007 by long-time independent editor/publishers and partners Diane Kistner and Robert S. King, the press incorporated as a nonprofit in 2012. A number of our editors are distinguished poets and authors in their own right, and we have been actively involved in the small press movement going back to the early seventies.

Our annual anthology, *FutureCycle*, combines poetry and flash fiction. The FutureCycle Poetry Book Prize and honorarium is awarded annually for the best full-length volume of poetry we publish in a calendar year. We are dedicated to giving all authors we publish the care their work deserves, making our catalog of titles the most distinguished it can be, and paying forward any earnings to fund more great books.

We've learned a few things about independent publishing over the years. We've also evolved a unique, resilient publishing model that allows us to focus mainly on vetting and preserving for posterity the most books of exceptional quality without becoming overwhelmed with bookkeeping and mailing, fundraising activities, or taxing editorial and production "bubbles." To find out more about what we are doing, come see us at www.futurecycle.org.